FINALLY AT PEACE

FINALLY AT PEACE

✦

A domestic violence survivor's story

Katie Kay

iUniverse, Inc.
New York Lincoln Shanghai

FINALLY AT PEACE
A domestic violence survivor's story

iUniverse books may be ordered through booksellers or by contacting:

iUniverse
2021 Pine Lake Road, Suite 100
Lincoln, NE 68512
www.iuniverse.com
1-800-Authors (1-800-288-4677)

ISBN-13: 978-0-595-34341-6 (pbk)
ISBN-13: 978-0-595-79108-8 (ebk)
ISBN-10: 0-595-34341-4 (pbk)
ISBN-10: 0-595-79108-5 (ebk)

Printed in the United States of America

Contents

ACKNOWLEDGEMENTS

Even though my story is, thank God, a short one; there are many people who I will always remain grateful to for helping me out of my living hell.

My two grown sons, Derek and Jason, for without them literally screaming to me on the telephone that night in late September 2003, screaming at me so that I would come to my senses, I reached the complete turning point at that moment and never looked back.

I am grateful to my parents, who tried in their own way to help me in June 2003.

I thank my sons' father, who helped me move, even though he didn't have to.

Thanks and blessing to all my friends from work who helped me find a place to live, gave me money and literally helped me move on a cold January day—my gratitude will never fade.

Thank you to those family and friends who listened to me on the phone and in person—thank you for not shutting me out, even after it appeared that I had shut you out.

Last but not least, to my current and permanent partner, for his love, understanding and patience with me as I continue to recover from PTSS; he has been directly responsible in helping me regain my trust in others, and realizing what true love really is. He has been a blessing in my life, and has made my life complete.

PREFACE

I grew up in Chicago during the 60's and 70's, graduating from a Catholic high school in 1976. My father was a police officer in a nearby suburb, and my mom was a homemaker until I reached the 7th grade, and then she only worked part time. I have one brother, 3 years younger than I. We grew up in a great neighborhood.

I did quite well in school, an A/B student and consider myself intelligent. I have been employed as an administrative assistant for a large corporation for the last 5 years, and have earned an outstanding reputation and the respect of my colleagues.

I am also a Pisces. Even though I am not deeply into astrology, I do believe astrology has a direct affect on one's life. I do believe that the characteristics of each sign described in astrology books are pretty accurate. I know that in my life it is accurate. Most Pisces people readily sympathize with anyone who is in dire straits. We always want to help someone who is in need, or in trouble. Our efforts will usually center around helping others, or helping the world become a better place somehow, even at our own inconvenience. We abhor violence and anything that upsets the very nature of things. This characteristic can easily be viewed as being naïve, or ignorant. My desire to help others has often resulted in someone taking advantage of me. My acceptance of people as a whole, and my ability to see the good in all people, *without keeping my healthy boundaries*, is a direct link to why I allowed myself to become involved with an abusive person, and allowed me return to my abuser once. I was too trusting of people, to accepting, too caring. I state these things in the past tense because I am no longer the person that I used to be in these ways.

I was married the first time in 1978 at the ripe old age of 20. This marriage lasted 20 years and produced my two wonderful sons, Derek and Jason. The marriage fell apart and we divorced in 1998. My sons lived with their dad in the house they grew up in, and I was on my own.

It took me quite a while to adjust to being "out of my normal world" being mom, taking care of the house, appointments, etc. I was married half of my life, so this was truly an adjustment. It wasn't easy at first, as I didn't reap any fluid monetary "rewards" from the divorce. Instead of allowing the situation to scare me, I took control of my life. I took a couple of classes at night to further sharpen my secretarial skills, and I routinely looked for a better job than the one I had at the time. I was determined to have a good life and realized that I wasn't going to be homeless, and that I wasn't helpless and could provide for myself. This is the drive and determination that later helped me get out of my abusive second marriage. I had the courage and strength I needed to "make it". You do too.

What I am not…I am not a psychologist or a counselor. My experience and education about domestic violence has helped me become a better person with healthier boundaries. Because I am not afraid to speak out against domestic violence, people in my circle know what I have been through and I have had many women come to me for help and advice. I use my resources to refer women to the professionals or agencies that will help them get back on their feet physically, mentally and financially.

1

Meeting My Abuser

What we don't know when we meet people of course, is how they really are. We need to form our relationships over time, get to know one another, see if we are comfortable with that person. *It is a known fact that abusers will move into a relationship very quickly, so as to "capture" their victim.*

I went to a concert with my girlfriend one warm August night. It was a beautiful night, the stars were shining and the warm breeze touched our faces as we walked into a small bar where a rock band was to start playing at 10:00pm. I was feeling great after having been to the pool that day, which always makes me feel relaxed and healthy. It was fairly crowded in the bar, but we managed to find a table and sat down. We ordered our drinks and shared our stories of what we did during the day. A couple of guys came by the table and struck up meaningless conversation. Just then, the band started to play and I became more interested in listening to the music than chatting. By the third song, about 20 people were up on the medium sized wooden dance floor dancing. My girlfriend turned to me and pointed to the dance floor and said "let's dance." As I was walking to the dance floor, I noticed a man sitting to the left of where I was walking, staring at me. He seemed to be with a group of five or six people. I looked at him, and noticed that he was quite good looking. He had shoulder length hair that was clean and combed back. He wasn't too thin or too heavy. As I passed him he smiled at me and I smiled back. As I danced, I realized that he was watching me. After the song was over, my girlfriend and I went to our table, and he again smiled at me and appeared to be interested in talking to me.

The band had belted out a couple of more songs and I was having a fun talking with the people at my table and listening to the music. Then, the band began a slow dance song.

The man who had been staring at me for most of the time I had been there began to walk over to where I was sitting. He bent his face over to my ear and spoke in a quiet tone into my ear.

"Hi, my name is Alan. Would you care to dance?" he asked.

"Sure" I said as I got up from my seat and followed him to the dance floor. I am 5'5" tall and he hovered above me at 6 feet. He put his arms around me and gently pulled me toward him. His cologne smelled like a woodsy smelling musk and I liked it. He was a wonderful dancer, moving us both smoothly around the dance floor. He asked me my name and told me how beautiful I looked.

"You are the only woman I see in this place."

He was quite charming and as we talked, I took a liking to his good sense of humor.

I would have never guessed by this first meeting, that this good looking, charming man was capable of the audacities that would come to pass.

Because I was impressed initially, I saw him again and again, thinking I was really getting to know this person. He had magnetism that drew people to him naturally. Very charming. He talked very easily to me about his life, his feelings, his issues, his wants and desires. I had never experienced this closeness with anyone in my life, and I liked it. I was not very close with my father, my first husband, and the couple of boyfriends I had been with. They really didn't know me, and I wanted a man to want to know me. This was not a bad thing, but it was my vulnerability and because he was fulfilling what I perceived as a need of mine at the time, I fell into what I now know as manipulating behavior. *I must state here, that most abusers are very charming, wonderful in a crowd or at a party, sometimes pillars of their community, and put on great façade outside of the home. Many times, when a victim finally tells her story of abuse to a family member or a friend, they don't believe her, because all they see is the charming, loving man who cares deeply for his girl-friend/wife.*

A painter by trade, he was very good at his job, and very creative. I liked that too. He treated me well, and was quite interested in me, which of course was flattering in the beginning. He was also, in the beginning, loving and unselfish. After a couple of months, he seemed to get into the depths of my person and knew how I was feeling without my having to tell him, which I of course liked because this is what I thought I wanted in my life, never realizing that he was in the process of getting me under his control. *This is a tactic that all abusers use to get control of their victims, and they are extremely good at it. This works very well on people who are kind hearted and caring.*

I learned that he had some health problems from earlier years of drug and alcohol use. He had previous problems with the law and family issues. Because he was giving me what I thought I wanted in a man, I dismissed his issues as trivial, as problems that can be overcome, with my help of course. Remember I am a Pisces, wanting to always help the downtrodden. I am also the person who always tried to figure things out and fix them.

In October, he asked me to marry him. I said yes. This was the biggest mistake of my life.

I married him 4 months after we met. I am sure my family and friends thought I had gone off the deep end…they knew me to be a levelheaded intelligent person. But of course, what could they do? Nothing. I had a civil ceremony in court with the bailiff as the witness, and that was it. We couldn't afford anything at the time. The plan was to get him on my health insurance, get him to feel better; we would buy a bigger place and live happily ever after. I would have fixed all his problems and then we would be happy. RIGHT. That was the plan. *I would like to note here, that this is another tactic abusers use to gain control of their victims…plan a future of love and happiness, with a willing participant, while knowing full and well that they will only live off of their partner (especially if they are addicts because addictive minds are always thinking of how to use other people for their own benefit). I unknowingly and unwittingly enabled him to use me and control me for his own gain. Being who I was, I just wanted to help this poor soul. Besides, I thought I loved him.*

It wasn't long before I found out what I had married. I was now his wife; his "property" and he tried to take total control of my life. How did he do this? How did I allow it to happen? *The reader needs to understand that, while dealing with day to day activities and life, and having little or no prior knowledge of domestic violence, and perhaps having witnessed domestic violence while growing up, victims get hooked into what they deem are loving relationships, wanting to figure out what is wrong, blaming themselves, and somehow believing that they can "fix" what is wrong and look forward to a better future. They believe that the abuser could change; they are constantly told by the abusers themselves of love and change during the honeymoon phase of the abusive cycle, which is discussed later in this book.*

2

Types of Abuse

Insane jealousy was one of Alan's most used abuses. He would imagine me having affairs with my boss, my co-worker, my ex-husband, neighbors, whomever. This was extremely maddening to me, as I am a devoted person when involved in a relationship or marriage. He knew me very well, to the point of almost knowing what I was thinking when I was thinking it. In the end I realized that this was one of the vehicles that enabled him to use his control over me…by knowing me so well, he knew exactly what to do or say to get to me.

I had no desire for any other man, and never gave him any reason to doubt that. But he would use his jealousy as a form of control and it drove me crazy. And he would go to extremes to try to prove himself right.

I took him to my office Christmas party, and in the beginning things were fine. After dinner, my boss was trying to get people to dance. He motioned our table to get up and dance, and Alan thought my boss was asking me in particular to dance. "Go ahead Katie, dance with him," he said, as he pushed me off of my chair!! I landed on the floor, unhurt, but totally embarrassed in front of my friends and coworkers. I ran to the bathroom, where my girlfriends ran in and asked me if I was ok. I could not believe the audacity of that man! That was only 3 weeks after we were married.

One night after I got home from work, he had somewhere to go. While he was gone, I was doing laundry. I would always fold my laundry on the bed. This particular night, I took my laundry into the bedroom, smoothed out the bedspread (the bed had not been made) and proceeded to dump the clean towels on the bed and fold them. He came home, looked at the bedspread smoothed out, and accused me of screwing the neighbor upstairs while he was gone. When I questioned him about it, why he would even think that, he said "because I positioned

5

the bedspread in such a way that I knew how I left it before I left. The bedspread's been moved, and you must have had so and so in this bed." This accusation was followed with name calling (you whore, slut, who do you think you are) and degradation (just look at you, all those stretch marks on your stomach, who the hell would want you anyway). I told him he was crazy, and he got this maniac look in his eyes and proceeded to forcefully pull my pants off and smell me for smells of another man. I was terrified that he was going to take his teeth and bite me, but he didn't. When he didn't smell anything, he backed off. I was totally in shock and confused (*this is what he wanted of course*).

As winter turned into spring, incidents like these began to happen more often and become more violent. By late spring I had a written list of incidents, dates, and injuries. Most of the incidents in my case and all other cases, are usually started over some imaginary affair or, in the abuser's mind, caused by the victim somehow. For example, when I was driving us around town one day doing errands, I came to a corner to make a left turn. I was looking at traffic to make sure I was clear to turn. He accused me of looking at some man in a truck to my left, and began calling me names and degrading me. Now, I wasn't looking at any man, I was observing traffic to make a left turn. Of course he didn't believe this, and he proceeded to punch me in the head and slap me in the face, screaming obscenities at me while I was driving! Can you imagine the horror of being beaten, let alone beaten while you are driving? My head and face hurt, and I was crying. I was infuriated so much that I reached over and smacked him while driving. I drove us home, but of course, the abuse didn't stop once we got home. There, it escalated to the point where he beat me in the head, knocked over the chair with me in it, and pulled the hair right out of my head. I could swear he gave me a slight concussion that evening. The next day I felt nauseous and sick. *Here I will note that most abusers will hit their victims where the bruises cannot be seen, usually in the head, stomach, back or buttocks. This keeps their use of control seen only by the victim. It is also good to note here how in control of themselves they really are, choosing where to hit their victim so it cannot be seen by others.*

He would call me at work 10 or 15 times a day, and if I wasn't at my desk, I was "missing". He would accuse me of screwing somebody in the supply room or some other outrageous accusation. It was the classic tactic of "if I don't see you, you must be doing something bad". This control over another is sick and absurd, and I'm glad I don't understand it, because if I did, I would feel just as sick.

By early summer, I had been hit in the head, hit on the side of the head which made my ears ring and my eyes see stars, had my hair pulled out of my head, had been literally kicked out of bed, kept up all night to "solve this once and for all", forcing me to miss the next days work. I had been called every name in the book, degraded, humiliated, doubted, you name it.

These incidents and many more, too many to mention here, always alternated with sincere sounding apologies, sometimes accompanied by real tears of remorse and sorrow. He wrote a wonderful love letter to me for Valentine's Day, expressing his love and "need" for me, his desire to always make me happy, because he "never met anyone like me and didn't want to lose me".

This is the cycle of abuse…the abusive incident is followed by apologies, and because the victim wants to believe this person who "loves" her, she accepts the apologies and hopes that things will be better in the future. Most victims will try to avoid any more incidents by trying to live their lives so as not to upset the abuser in any way, therefore perpetrating another abusive incident. Many victims tell me they feel like they are walking on eggshells. Until we are aware and educated about domestic violence, we are unaware that, no matter what we do to avoid another incident, it will NEVER work because the abuser will always find a rhyme or reason to exert his power and control over the victim. Victims need to understand that they do not cause the abuse and therefore cannot stop it. This is the first major step in leaving the abusive relationship.

The abuser makes a choice to control the victim and truly can control himself, but he doesn't want to. It feels good for him to have power over, since he is so insecure and unsure of his own self and self worth. Also, releasing anger is a stress reliever for them, and like an addiction, feels so good that they have to do it again, and again, and again. Victims need to realize that there is NOTHING they can do to help this; victims did nothing to start it and they absolutely cannot fix it. One time my abuser asked me for help. "Please help me Katie" he said through a crying fit and tears. I told him that I was not qualified to help him, that he needed professional help.

One very warm evening in June, we went out to dinner. He had been working and it appeared he had been drinking on the job. I felt the intense aura of stress he emitted when he was ready to blow up. We ate dinner, and our conversation once again escalated into anger for no apparent reason. During our conversation, he asked me where I was when he called me at work. I said that I had gone out of the office to purchase some needed items for an event we were going to have at work. This infuriated him, the fact that I was out of the office instead of sitting at my desk where "I should be". In his mind, I must have been out seeing another man. This of course was so totally ridiculous I couldn't believe it! We left the restaurant, and he insisted that he drive. Once in the car, he continued yelling at me, telling me what a whore I was, who would want me, etc. etc.

"You know what I'm gonna do with you? I'm gonna drop you off in the street, where all the niggers could get you, you little whore."

The town he referred to was very poor, downtrodden, full of crime and plain and simply, a bad neighborhood. He was driving in that direction, and going to let me out of my own car there!! Imagine the fear that I had, along with extreme anger at this man for wanting to not only endanger my life but also throw me out of my own car!! I am sure you have heard of the "fight or flight" reaction to fear—I knew what I had to do. As he was driving down the street, traffic came to a stop and as the car was stopped, I jumped out! I ran into the first public building that I came to and hid in the bathroom, as I knew he was going to follow me. I held myself up by the sink, literally shaking from the intense fear I felt raging through my body. I looked into the mirror at myself. My hair was all messed up because he had been pulling at it. Makeup was smeared around my eyes from the tears that had been streaming down my face. I looked past my face and behind me, the mirror reflected part of the outside lobby, where an older man was sitting, probably waiting for somebody. I heard the door open, and saw through the mirror, this older man looking at whom I knew was Alan as though he was looking at a maniac, and he was! He must have looked around for me for a few minutes, and then left. I was so scared I was shaking uncontrollably. I had to gather my wits, and decide what to do. I washed my face, and decided to use the payphone in the lobby to call my parents for help.

I must have sounded like a babbling idiot, calling them from a payphone, telling them I was in trouble, and giving them the wrong information, that I was at a bowling alley, when in fact I was in the local hockey rink. They phoned police, who of course couldn't find me, and they called my aunt, who called the number of the pay phone where I was, asking me my location. My family was scared for me and angry that this had happened to me. But they were 30 miles away and couldn't get there at the time. They also thought the best thing to do was phone police who could help me right away. The whole scene is a foggy memory to me, but in the end, I went home. I wasn't going to let him get away with this. I was going home to my condo; it was my condo, and I was going to kick him out.

Going home was another big mistake.

By the time I got home, he was there. I was screaming and crying, telling Alan he was a complete crazy person, and I wanted him out of the house! This further infuriated him, and a physical fight ensued. He attacked me with the force of his 6 foot, 200 pound body, and I tried with all of my strength to fight him off. He came after me and forced me to the floor, hitting me in the face and head. I made a fist and hit him back. He put his hand over my mouth because I was screaming, and I thought he was going to suffocate me. He didn't of course, because then I wouldn't be around for him to abuse anymore! What fun would that have been? I managed to get both of my feet to my chest, and with all my strength I put my feet to his chest and pushed him away from me. I got up from the floor and ran to the door to leave. He came after me, grabbed me and with one hand and with his force, he thrust my forehead into the corner of wall. I immediately felt a big knot on my head; I was dizzy and I felt disoriented. I don't remember how, but I got out the door and started running. I could hear him yelling after me to come back into the house. I staggered down the street about a mile, came to a nursing home, rang the doorbell and asked the nurse who answered the door to call police. The look on her face told me that the sight of me must have scared her half to death!

A couple of squad cars arrived. The 3 officers took one look at me and called an ambulance. I was treated right there and refused to go to the hospital. They made a report, which I still had. They asked me if I wanted to press charges. I said, "No if I do that he will really kill me". *I would like to note here, this is very typical of a victim in distress, and because of fear of the abuser, still trying to deflate any situation to avoid further retaliation. Also, I mentioned that I still have the copy of the report. Keep all documentation; keep all reports and notes so you can build a case.*

One of the police officers said, "Katie, I don't need your permission to arrest him. I'm going over there (to the condo) and put him in custody." With that, he left with another officer, leaving me with the third officer and the ambulance men. I signed a release, as I was not going to the hospital (although now I wish I had, because it would have been more documentation against him). He was arrested and charged with domestic battery. I went home, and for the first time in months, felt like maybe I could sleep in peace.

3

Leaving Home and Going Back

One of the worst things in the world is being made to feel you need to leave the place you live, the place you call home. I bought my condo in July 2000, remodeled the kitchen, and decorated it and made it my own. I was proud of my little postage stamp on earth, and I didn't want anyone telling me or otherwise making me leave it. You really don't leave a place you like living in unless you decide to do so on your own, for whatever your own reasons are. It was my place, I owned it, and I didn't want to leave it. Not for any reason other than if I decided to move to a larger place.

I asked my parents if I could stay with them for a few days to get my wits about me and decide on a plan of action. Of course they said yes and welcomed me with open arms. My mom washed my clothes for me; they fed me and basically supported me for a few days. I appreciated this tremendously. I was literally beat up, felt like I got run over by a Mack truck, and needed the time away from my condo and supportive people to be with. They will never know to this day how much that meant to me.

One week later, I returned to my condo. Alan had been in contact with me, crying, apologetic, and supposedly in a state of mind of understanding where he went wrong, and he promised me he would NEVER EVER hit or hurt me again. He literally got down on his knees, with streams and streams of tears running down his face, begging my forgiveness and honestly, praying to God right in front of me to take him back. I did. This was the second biggest mistake of my life.

This is a classic ploy that abusers use to pull the victim back in under their control. It works very well on anyone basically, anyone who has any feelings at all, let alone not knowledgeable about abuse, abusers and how they operate. Abusive people can turn their feelings on and off like a faucet, literally. If you have ever felt as though your partner is a Dr. Jekyll/Mr. Hyde, believe me this is a classic example. They can switch from one mode to the other exactly when they need to, when it will benefit THEM the most. They do not care about you and are totally incapable of love or feelings for you, unless it benefits them and their insecurity about themselves. If you feel this may be happening in your relationship, please step back and take a look at how your partner turns on and off at exactly the right times to tug on your heart when need be. When they are feeling comfortable with the relationship, that is when they take control again, and the cycle of abuse continues on.

This "calm" lasted about 4 weeks, and I truly unknowingly believed this man knew what he did wrong and was atoning for his sins. Because we were "trying again", I never went to court on the domestic battery charge which was a huge mistake. He got off because there was no complaining witness in court. Had I gone to court, I could have had him put in jail for quite some time.

One month had passed without incident, but soon I was feeling a certain, familiar, tension in the air. The cycle was continuing, the only difference was that there was a longer hiatus between incidents.

One hot evening in August I was cooking dinner, and he had gone outside. He returned steaming and furious as though he had just had an argument with someone outside. When I asked what was wrong, he answered "your boyfriend is outside in the parking lot in his purple truck". Of course I was shocked, I had no boyfriend and knew no one at all with a purple truck. He slurred at me "you fucking whore, who do you think you are" and smacked me in the face. I looked at him in total shock. I said, "You hit me". Because this was against our new covenant, he knew he lost it, which made him more furious. He pushed me out the patio door and into the railing that was around my patio. That push into the railing cut my right arm and bruised my right leg. I ran to the parking lot and saw 2 women walking into the back door of the building. I asked them, "is this your purple truck?" The younger of the two women said it was her truck. I asked her to come into my condo and tell that to my husband, and God bless her, she did. She was with her mom, who lived in the condo next to mine, and she was visiting her. She instinctively knew what was going on, either that or her mom had heard some of our fights and had told her daughter about them. They both came into the condo with me, and she looked him in the eye and said "that is my purple truck. My husband bought it for me for my birthday last year. I've been married

35 years and he is good to me". Alan started to rant about me having affairs and such, and they looked at him like he was out of his mind, which of course he was. They then turned to me with pity in their eyes, said good night and left.

He could never "catch" me doing anything wrong, and this made him even angrier and more jealous than ever.

Here I must note that this is a perfect example of what I have heard many women say, and I at one time felt the same way. "No matter what I do, no matter how I act or how "good" I am, it's never good enough". This completely endorses the fact that the abusive person's behavior has nothing to do with how his partner acts. No matter what she does, she must understand that she is not the "cause" of his abusive behavior, she can't control it (only he can and does when the need arises), and she can't "fix" it, no matter how hard she tries. It must be understood that this is not a "marital" problem, as many abusers claim and would like their partner to believe. Remember, they cannot take blame or fault for their actions and will turn the blame onto their partners—unless they are trying to "make up" for what they have done (this is when they are "reeling" the partner back into the relationship). I've said it before but it is good to note here that this is very classic ploy. It works very well on the loving and empathetic person.

I completely doubted his sincerity, knowing full well I was in a bad situation and needed to get out fast. I had started to look for information and help on the internet regarding abusive relationships. I had read and read and read everything I could about it. I filled my head with education and information about abuse and abusive people and relationships. I truly believed that I was reading about my very own life on the internet. I felt like I ran into a brick wall, and my entire being was paralyzed and shocked about what I was learning about abuse. I felt stupid and used, totally drained and sick to my stomach after reading about the facts of my life, and countless other's lives as well on the internet.

My friends at work were very supportive during this time. I was beginning to open up and talk, and they would talk back. They helped me tremendously during this time and beyond, as I will write about in later chapters.

4

Getting Rid of the Devil

One cool night in late September, once again Alan exploded in a fit of rage that at this writing I cannot even remember what it was about. Believe me when I tell you, it was more of the same, the name calling, the accusations of infidelity, the stupid childish fighting that he so came to love to use against me on the drop of a dime because he needed to explode.

Violence is a cycle, and the need to explode is a part of the cycle. It is a noted fact that most abusers actually get off sexually with the explosion of their temper. They need the explosion, the cool off period, and then the cycle starts all over again. Imagine being trapped in a relationship where this is what is happening constantly. The cycle can last as short as days or as long as a year. But it is there, and it is constant, and it will never change.

A physical fight ensued as an end result of this need to explode. This lasted well into the night. The next morning he was still angry as hell and I was scared as hell. I didn't sleep all night, wondering if he would just kill me in the middle of the night. I got up in the morning to his seething verbal attacks. I didn't say a word. I went to the bathroom and looked at my face. My left eye was blackened, the whites of both eyes were red, I imagine due to broken blood vessels from being hit in the head. I had six other bruises on my body from being thrown around the kitchen of my condo. I washed my face, looked at myself in the mirror, and I said to myself "THIS IS IT". NO MORE.

I got dressed haphazardly and ran out of the house. I knew he had a job he was going on, and I hoped he was going to leave for it soon. I went to a restaurant near work, sat down and thought. And thought. And thought. I felt paralyzed yet I knew I couldn't fall apart, I had to do something soon. I decided to go to work for an hour, to let people see me because I may need them in court as witnesses. I truly am sorry for what I put my friends through that day. I looked awful. I wanted them to see that…I was beginning to build my case. This time, I wasn't turning back.

Now that I had witnesses, I called my house. No one answered. I went back home, and with all the strength I had left, I packed every stitch of clothing, every shoe, every item I could find, I packed everything of his. I put them out on my patio. I called him at the job he was at. I told him to come and get his stuff, and to never come back here again. I swore and screamed and yelled until I had a sore throat. Then I left the house, because I knew better. I knew that if I had stayed, that maggot might have very well beaten me to death. I left for 6 hours; I wandered around the local mall, drove around, anything just to stay away while he picked up his stuff. When I finally went back, he and his stuff were gone. I was relieved. But not at peace. I wouldn't be at peace for a while. Even though it was over, it wasn't over.

5

Continued Abuses

Alan had taken his stuff and moved to a family member's house, nearby. This man would not stop calling me both at work and at home. He would leave countless messages for me, asking me to be his friend, begging for forgiveness, telling me of his "love" for me, and then finally "admitting" that he didn't blame me for what I was doing. On the contrary, he stalked me, left me angry messages, and be walking down my street at 6:15 in the morning when I was leaving for work. He would go back and forth, Dr. Jekyll and Mr. Hyde, and I never knew which one was going to call or show up next.

To compound things and make matters worse, I had developed some female health issues in November that needed attention. I had to have 2 biopsies done, one called an endometrial biopsy and the other being a breast biopsy. These procedures were both extremely uncomfortable, and the added stress of wondering if I had cancer was almost more than I could bear. I truly thank God that in the middle of December I found out that I was going to be ok, but in the meantime I had gone from 123 pounds down to 107 pounds. The stress and emotional turmoil were starting to take their toll on my health. Although this was happening to me, I knew I had to stay strong and move forward, always keeping in mind my goal to get away from this maggot that was draining my very existence.

One Saturday morning in December, after I knew I didn't have cancer, about 6:00am, I was half asleep. What is that noise? It sounded like my door being pried open! I jumped out of bed and began walking down the hallway. There he was, his tall dark figure coming down the hallway right at me. I began to shake with fear, wondering what would happen next.

"Who's in there?" he asked me pointing to my bedroom.

I yelled at him "no one, who the hell would be in there?"

He repeated the question and pushed past me to go into my bedroom to see who was in my bed. Of course no one was in there, and he sighed a sigh of relief, and wouldn't you know it, immediately put on a pouty, sorry face and began apologizing. I could smell beer on his entire person. He had been out all night, and while on his way home, he passed my house (as usual) and saw a truck in my parking lot that he didn't recognize. Of course he thought that this was someone I was seeing, became suspicious (as usual) and broke in. I was furious! I was screaming at him now, how dare he break into my house, how dare he do this.

"You are a f****g criminal! Get out".

He wanted to come back later and fix the door frame that he had so easily broken away from the wall. He was insistent and beginning to get angry because I wasn't buying into his sorry act. I couldn't take it anymore, and I think if I had a weapon I might have used it.

I knew this wouldn't stop until I moved away, and I knew it wouldn't even stop after that. I had already begun looking for condos and getting pre-approved for a mortgage in November. I had told my children and my friends that I was going to move after the holidays. I did end up moving, but not the way I had intended.

6

Breaking Free

Very early in January I came home from work at about 5:30pm, and as I was entering the back door to my building, I saw him up ahead, leaving my condo. He saw me, and, like a child caught doing something wrong, proceeded out the front door in a rush. Once again, I was enraged. The man was in my condo!! I ran to the front door, and I called his name, and asked him what the heck he was doing in my condo. This was a big mistake, just as the entire relationship was a big mistake. He came back into the little front lobby, and proceeded to lie to me, telling me that he wasn't in my condo, telling me he was just in the building "warming up" getting out of the January cold. I knew I had made a mistake by even approaching the subject because of course all he would do was lie. I told him to just get out, but now he wouldn't leave! Now he was going to stay and torture me some more. He asked me if he could come in, and when I told him no, I had an appointment, he begged me "just for 5 minutes".

"I just want to talk to you. I miss you."

I told him no, but he would not leave. He just wouldn't. *I'd like to note here, that when the victim finally takes action to leave the situation, the abuser will do anything to talk to or see the victim. "Just for 5 minutes" is a very common and classic ploy used on a regular basis by these people.*

He followed me into my condo, sat at the kitchen table, and began to berate me for thinking that he was in my condo, who did I think I was, how could I be like that, etc. Blaming me again for what he had done. I felt the familiar tension rising, and again told him to leave, that I had an appointment. He unwillingly agreed to leave, but only if I gave him a ride because after all, it was freezing cold outside. I agreed to the ride just to get him out and away from me. Once we arrived at the house, he decided it would be fun to terrorize me and not get out of the car. He said he'd come to my appointment with me, and when I said no he couldn't, he of course became enraged. "Why not?" he asked me. I told him it was a counseling appointment, as I was already in counseling, and that just gave him more ammunition to further berate me.

I got out of the car and started walking towards the door of the house to ask for help. I was going to ask someone to call the police, but as I was walking up to the door, he bolted out of the car, and yanked on my arm so hard I almost fell to the ground. He told me to stay away from the door, and began yelling at me, terrible things that I don't even remember anymore. All I wanted to do was get away from this maniac. I got my senses together and realized, hey, he's out of the car! I jumped in the car and sped away from there as fast as I could.

I went home, terrified, trying to think straight. I knew I had to leave, and this infuriated me. I sat down at my kitchen table, trying to think of what to do next, when the phone rang. It was him of course.

"Why do you lie to me?" he asked me. "You are not at your appointment".

I told him that I was now too late for my appointment, thanks to him. Of course he was still enraged from earlier, even more so now.

"Don't f**k with me Katie. You are really pissing me off with your lies and deceit. I am really mad. You better leave that condo while you could still walk and drive a car you f*****g whore."

I hung up on him. My heart was pounding. My hands were sweating and my body was literally shaking with fear. I ran to the bathroom, and looking in the mirror, I gathered my thoughts. I knew what I had to do to basically save my life. He was coming over, and I truly believed that he would kill me. I packed a small bag, and called the police for protection. When the police got there, which thank God was within 5 minutes of my calling them, I told them what happened. I asked them to escort me to my car, which they did, and I left my home, never to return to live or sleep there ever again.

I was not turning back—I had made that mistake once before, and I pride myself on the fact that I never make the same big mistakes twice. I wasn't going to do it this time either.

I went to a hotel that I use to put up my out of town guests from work. It cost me $100 that night, but I didn't care. I was safe. I took a bath and decided that my next move was to get a cheaper place to live until I found an apartment somewhere. What a profoundly terrible feeling it is to own a home and have no permanent place to live! Now I was really angry, infuriated and I was on a mission to get my life back together again, but I knew I needed help.

The next day I went to work and told my friends the predicament I was in. They already knew what I was going through, and were ready, willing and able to help me. I thank God for them and all those who stood beside me during those times of my need.

One of my girlfriends found a hotel I could stay in that had weekly rates until I could find an apartment. I "moved in" to this hotel. I paid for 7 days, and hoped that I could find something more permanent in that short period of time.

I had only packed a small bag in my haste to leave my condo, so after 2 days I needed more clothes for work and a few more personal items, since I was never going back home. Two days later I took a half-day vacation and returned to my condo to get more of my things. On the way there, I stopped at the police station and requested an escort.

When we arrived at my condo, the police officer took my key, opened my door and announced his presence. There was Alan, waiting for me!! He must have been there for 2 days now, just waiting for me to come back. I must tell you, I completely lost it! I felt such a surge of anger and rage; I began to scream expletives at this criminal maggot. "What are you doing in my house? How did you get in here? You so and so" and so forth, I just let it loose. The officer needed to gain control of the situation and told me that I needed to leave the building. I remember hearing him asking Alan what he was doing in my house. Of course Alan answered in his most charming, sweet and calm tone, "I was worried about my wife, officer. I wondered where she was and when she was coming home". The audacity of that man!! He didn't care about anything except getting his hands around my throat and "punishing" me for "leaving him".

The officer again asked me to leave the building, which I did. I went across the street to my neighbor's, who took me in and calmed me down. A back up officer came, they arrested him for criminal trespass and took him to the station. I went to the station afterwards and signed a complaint and got a court date. I wasn't going to let this maggot get off of anything anymore.

I must note here, that the police were very good with the situation, however what I am about to convey next will confirm the fact that abusive people are very cunning, charming, and could get anyone to believe anything they say and have things slanted their own way. Depending on the nature of the people in the specific law enforcement entities in your area, you may experience difficulties receiving help from people who are supposed to uphold the law.

7

Police are People Too

The fact is that law enforcement agencies have not been educated on the subject of domestic violence until the mid 1980's. And the education process is a slow one, and not always updated or part of the officers ongoing education, like target practice is. They are required to have target practice and participate in seminars occasionally, however the educational seminars on domestic violence are not always a part of the program on a regular basis. This results in newly hired officers being uneducated on the subject. Realistically in the 21st century, they have become extremely more educated than in the past, but again, this depends on the area that you live in.

Where I lived, most of the officers understood the tangled web of domestic violence. The story I am about to tell is just one of many hiccups in society.

I went to the police station to sign the complaint. One of the detectives came to me with the complaint, which I signed. He went back behind closed doors, and came out about 15 minutes later. He looked at me and said, "I know this may sound stupid, but he asked me to ask you for the $100 bond money. Will you bond him out?" What this poor detective went through next is a form of abuse in itself. I totally lost my temper, and told the detective to tell that maggot "FU" and I held up my finger to animate the gesture. I once again lost it and he looked at me with a scared, "oh my god" look on his face. He told me he understood my position, and reminded me of the many women who in fact bond their abusers out of jail. After my tirade, he realized I wasn't going to be one of those women. He apologized and went back behind closed doors. I got a copy of the complaint and started to leave the police station.

Just then, a younger police officer working on the case came out from the back. He asked me a question. He said that Alan told him that we had just taken the

Christmas tree down, we were doing fine, we made love recently, etc. Alan got this guy believing in him. I looked the officer straight in the eye.

"Are you married?"

"No"

"Do you have a girlfriend?"

"Yes I do."

I asked if they lived together and he said no.

"If you make love to your girlfriend on Sunday, does that mean she has the right to break into your house on Tuesday?"

Of course a look of surprise came over him because now I put things in perspective for him in regards to his own life.

"Well, no of course not" he sheepishly said, realizing that he should have known that in the first place.

"I have been divorcing this monster since October, he does not belong in my house, he is a criminal and an abuser. Any concern you have for him is stupid," I said as I proceeded to walk out the door.

Generally speaking, the awareness and education on domestic violence is now penetrated throughout the law enforcement agencies more than it used to be back in the 1980's. Quite a number of the officers, detectives, states attorneys and judges have themselves experienced some form of domestic abuse in their own personal lives and understand it to some degree. The tolerance level for this sort of crime has become very low. However, there are still some people in law enforcement and the judicial system who are not willing or able to see domestic violence for what it is, let alone the average victim trapped in a situation. No wonder this continues to be an ongoing societal problem.

The next day, I took a vacation day from work and I spent the entire day in court getting an order of protection. By 10:00 that night, I had three phone messages left on my cell phone from Alan.

"I'm out, and you're in trouble. You are not that far away from me you stupid c**t. I'll be there soon".

I was exhausted from spending the whole day in court. I was back in my hotel room listening to this maniac ranting on my cell phone. Alan's voice on my phone sent shock waves through my body. I was so tired but the sound of his voice sent shivers up my spine. I called the police station and reported the messages and their content. They told me to come in so they could make another report. Even though I was so exhausted and stressed out, I agreed to do the long ride to the police station. I knew I needed all the paperwork I could get on this maggot. I got there at 10:40pm. The detectives listened to the messages, wrote up a report and called him at home, and surprisingly he answered the phone. He was informed that there was an order of protection against him and that he was never to call me or have any contact with me again. I got back to the hotel at 12:30am.

The next few days were spent finding an apartment. I was living in a hotel and I had to find something more permanent. My emotions were extreme; I had explicit hate for this man. I felt extreme fear for my safety and began to contemplate purchasing a firearm for my protection, although I never did.

My girlfriend from work helped me find an apartment, my friends from work and my ex husband helped me move. My sons were there too after work, helping me move my mattress in and moving boxes down 2 flights of stairs into the basement. I truly thank God for all of their help, because believe me, I feel that this was the fastest move in recorded history, and I couldn't have done it without them.

Now I had a mortgage payment and a rent payment. I was also paying a lawyer for the divorce, and my situation, even though I was trying to make it better, was getting worse financially. I prayed to God to help me through all of this, and it was prayers and the help of my sons and friends, and my stubbornness and determination that eventually got me through it all. In the meantime, I found out later, he had been calling my boss and a co-worker, thinking I was staying with them, and threatening them with bodily harm.

Abusers will use the friends and family of their victim when they cannot readily get to their victim. This is classic behavior of abusive people. When they feel they are losing control of their victim, they will move to the victim's family, pets, friends, personal items, children, etc. If you feel your children, pets or family and friends are being threatened, you must continue to stay away from the abuser even though you may feel like going back to protect your children, family, friends or pets. Stay away and use the laws in your state or country to assist you. You cannot let him gain control once again, as the cycle will just repeat itself.

8

A Cold Hard Winter

I had literally become a recluse in the apartment that I moved into. Even though I did feel a bit safer where I was as opposed to being in my condo, I was terrified of going out after dark, which in the Midwestern United States during the winter is about 5:00 pm. I stayed in, night after night, weekend after weekend, looking out the window to see if he was coming to get me. I slept on the couch, paranoid, feeling that if I slept there, I could hear the door open if someone tried to get in. I lived in total fear, thinking he was going to come after me sooner or later. I cursed him in my mind every night, and I thanked God every morning that I woke up alive. I was now down to 104 lbs.

Even though Alan was informed he was not allowed to contact me by any means, he would call me at work. He called several times in January. It was during this time that he was also calling my boss and male co-worker threatening them with bodily harm, thinking I was staying with them. I went to court and had a warrant signed by the judge in his chambers for violation of order of protection. His bond was set at $5000.

Once you have decided to leave the situation permanently, you must take every avenue to build paperwork against your abuser. Do not let them get away with any violations of court orders, do what you must to document their actions in the court system. It will help you in the long run to put your abuser in jail. Unfortunately, they will not stay in jail and someday be released. You will be notified of their release, and you will want to attend the appeal hearing. Do all you can to keep them in jail, for when they get out, they will come back to you, or find another victim to abuse.

I continued to go to work, come home and stay in my apartment after dark. We didn't have caller ID on our phones at work, so when my business phone rings, I have to answer it. I cringed every time it rang.

He called me at work in early February.

"Yeah, why do you keep sending the cops over here?"

I of course hung up. I know now that the police were there to try to serve him divorce papers, which he kept dodging. They must have managed to do so, because I was informed a few days later that I had a divorce date—another trip to court. I had already had court dates set up to get my order of protection extended, and a court date for the criminal trespass charge.

My weight was continuing to plummet and my anger and frustration with what my life had become was taking its toll on me. Night after night I was going to sleep on the couch, listening for the door to open and him being there to get me. Morning after morning I would pray to God and thank him for allowing me another day.

It was a Sunday morning when I got a phone call on my cell phone at 5:20am. I heard the phone ring, got up to see who it was. It was the police station! The sergeant left a message on my cell phone to return his call. Great! I thought to myself. What did he do now, break into my condo, or maybe worse, burn the place down? I didn't know what to think about this early morning phone call.

I returned the sergeant's call promptly. This is what he told me:

"Your husband has been in an accident, and unfortunately he did not survive. I am sorry to have to tell you this on the phone, however I know you have moved away and I have no other way to contact you."

I was silent. I couldn't speak. I became paralyzed in thought.

I said, "Could you repeat that please?" And he did. For the second time, he repeated to me that Alan had been found face down in the snow at 3:00 in the morning, having been hit by a pickup truck. He did not survive the accident and had been pronounced dead a short time ago.

My first feeling was one of relief, relief that he could not ever come and get me again! I actually felt not only relief, but happy. But then, I felt guilty for feeling relieved and happy. I won't go into it here, but I must say that I have never experienced more conflicting emotions in all of my life. I spent the rest of the day crying, crying both from relief, happiness, and shock all combined. The feelings I had were so contradictory to each other, so unlike me to feel relief that someone was dead, and this was it, and it was final, and I didn't have to look over my shoulder anymore, didn't have to attend court dates, didn't have to live in fear. It was quite overwhelming to be honest, but I felt lucky to say the least. This man would never bother me again.

I am fortunate that I did not have to go identify the body, as most "next of kin" need to do. The police knew my situation and told me to just stay home. I wouldn't have done it anyway; I was trying to divorce this man and ran from him. The last thing I needed to do was play the role of "wife".

I was due to go out of town the next day on business for a few days. I needed to make huge decisions in a very short period of time. I knew that whatever decisions I made, I had to live with them the rest of my life. By 8:00 that night, I had decided to go out of town and leave the whole thing alone. I packed haphazardly; I felt like I was in a fog. The next morning I left with my co-workers and was out of town for 4 days. He was buried by the time I returned.

9

Finally At Peace

When I returned from my business trip, I found out that members of his family had tried to contact me at work in regards to the funeral. I don't know if they were doing it out of respect for my position as his wife, or if they just wanted money, but I never returned anyone's calls.

The following week, I took a couple of "funeral days" off of work, which I legitimately had coming. I had saved the obituary from the newspaper and knew the cemetery where he was buried. I drove to the cemetery and went inside the office and inquired as to where his body was. The nice man behind the counter gave me a map and told me how to get to his grave. "It's the only fresh one out there".

It was a cold day and there was some snow on the ground. I drove around the cemetery and at first I couldn't locate the grave. I drove around a curve, and I saw machine tracks in the snow going up a hill. This must be the grave, I thought to myself. I parked my car, zipping my jacket as I got out and followed the tracks up the hill. The tracks led to a fresh mound of dirt.

I just stood there for a minute. I stared down at the grave, but I didn't cry, I felt emotionless. I took out a red piece of construction paper on which I had written in black marker, "My husband, my abuser...I hope you are finally at peace". I stuck it in the dirt, and walked away.

I was finally at peace.

REFLECTIONS

I have gone through counseling and have met many wonderful women who not only have helped me through my pain but also have become my good friends. I only hope that my story, and my education and knowledge that I have gained have helped them as well.

My reason for writing this book is twofold; number one, if I have helped just one woman come to a realization about her abusive relationship, if I have helped just one woman come to terms with herself and leave and never turn back, and move on to a better life, then the turmoil it took me to write this book will be well worth the effort.

Number two; it was therapeutic to me to write this book. I didn't have to write it, and at times it was extremely difficult to do. Writing this book made me relive the audacities that were a part of my life. It honestly hurt. At the same time, it helped me bring closure to a short but traumatizing part of my life that I never will forget. I have moved on to a better life for having lived it. And you could too.

Once we realize what we have been through, what we had put up with and what we have lost in ourselves, we need to make a promise to ourselves to never, ever allow anyone to do this to us again. We need to remain cognizant of our demand for respect with love if we want to have a healthy loving relationship that is nurturing, kind, caring and loving mutually. We need to demand this of not only ourselves but of those around us. We need to relinquish those relationships that do not offer us these things, and move on to those that do. We need to understand that anyone we meet could be potential danger to us and proceed with caution, while learning to allow ourselves to trust again. This in itself is a tremendous feat, trusting without fear, while being cautious.

Trust, love and respect are earned, not a given, and our healthy boundaries will avail us of people around us who will do just that.

I am currently in a permanent, loving, trusting and healthy relationship with my boyfriend. He would never think of hurting me, we respect each other, and it feels good to feel good. You can have this too.

MY PERSONAL THOUGHTS AND HOPE FOR VICTIMS

Statistically, one out of every 3 people in the United States population are abusive. I believe it is more like half. No wonder this issue is so widespread and out of hand! Every other person that I have spoken to on the subject has either been through an abusive situation themselves, or knows someone who has.

I have not included every incident that had happened to me in this book, because I didn't want this book to be a "cry" session, I wanted it to be educational examples of the audacities that abuse victims and survivors can relate to.

I, and many women like me, are living proof that you can and are able to be a survivor of domestic violence. It is a hard road to travel, but what is your other option? It is living daily with the threat of someone hurting or possibly killing you. As you know, this is no way to live, and you deserve much better. There are many sources and resources to aid you in your plan for a better life.

The first thing one must do is understand the cycle of domestic violence. It happens in four distinct stages:

1. The tension building stage. This is the stage when the abuser starts to get angry, and if there is nothing to be angry about, the abuser will generally create an imaginary affair or falsely accuse the victim of some wrongdoing to justify his anger.

2. The "acting out" stage. This is the stage when any type of abuse occurs, be it verbal, physical, sexual, emotional or otherwise.

3. The "honeymoon" stage. This includes apologies from the abuser for his behavior, promises that it will never happen again, and statements of reform. This stage usually also includes placing the blame of the behavior on the victim and minimizing any injuries that may have occurred.

4.   Calm stage. This is the calm period of time before the cycle begins again. The abuser acts like the abuse never happened, and may shower the victim with gifts and "acts of kindness".

Once the cycle of violence is understood, victims are usually able to realize that they do not cause this, cannot fix it, and it will never change. EVER. So my plea to victims is this, *please get out.*

HELPFUL SOURCES OF INFORMATION

Every state in the United States has agencies and shelters to aid victims and their children. There are agencies in the U.K. as well. Contact the county or township in which you live for further information.

Another source of help is the United Way.

The internet is the largest source of information on the subject of domestic violence that I have found. If you would like to read more about domestic violence, here are some very informative and helpful sites:

www.survivorsofdv.com
www.hiddenhurt.com
www.web-street.com/thingsarelookingup
www.recovery-man.com

There are other books besides this one that are extremely helpful. You can find them on the website Rhiannon3.net

HEALING...YOUR OWN NEW JOURNEY

The healing process takes time and courage. Most victims of domestic violence and other crimes experience a great deal of trauma, and suffer symptoms of Post Traumatic Stress Syndrome. You can find more information on PTSS on the websites mentioned previously, and in your counseling sessions. Some symptoms of PTSS include insomnia, nightmares, excessive lethargy, loss of libido, inability to trust one's own judgment or trust in others, anxiety, and heightened reflex actions to movements around you.

The things that have helped me personally the most were getting educated on the subject and viewing it and accepting it for what it really is. I also took great comfort in prayer, and taking care of myself in small ways, like lounging in the bathtub or buying myself a new shirt to wear. It also helped me to talk to others about my experiences, whether it was in counseling or in other arenas, such as at work or with friends. As embarrassed as one may feel about discussing their personal domestic violence situation, I found that every other person I spoke to either went through similar experiences, or knew someone who had. This in itself allowed me to realize that I was not crazy, or stupid, and that this issue is such a widespread social dilemma is an understatement.

I encourage counseling, both one on one and group, and taking good care of yourself. You will find your own ways to cope and heal, take all the time you need. After all, you deserve it.

CLOSING

In this book I have referred to the abuser as being male, and the victim as being female. However, the truth is that women abuse too. There are battered men out there, albeit the percentages are smaller but this doesn't take away from the fact or ease their pain. Domestic violence exists in homosexual and lesbian relationships as well. There is also child abuse and abuse of the elderly. No matter what type of abuse it is, it is a huge societal problem that exists all over the world, and the efforts to control it, and the laws in place, are just not enough. Awareness, education and involvement on everyone's part is the key to the beginning of reform and change, so that we might all someday live in peace.

978-0-595-34341-6
0-595-34341-4

Printed in the United States
118368LV00004B/245/A